MAIDENHEAD
A Pictorial History

Boulter's Lock, early this century

MAIDENHEAD
A Pictorial History

Luke Over (signature)

Luke Over

Phillimore

1990

Published by
PHILLIMORE & CO. LTD.
Shopwyke Hall, Chichester, Sussex

ISBN 0 85033 730 5

Printed and bound in Great Britain by
BIDDLES LTD.
Guildford, Surrey

This book is dedicated to the late TOM MIDDLETON
a good friend and historical journalist who died in 1989.
In the many years that he was editor of the Maidenhead Advertiser
he recorded history as it occurred
and contributed much to our knowledge of Maidenhead's past.

List of Illustrations

Acknowledgements

The author is very grateful to the following people who have helped in the production of this book: Mrs. Patricia Curtis, Reference Librarian, and Mr. Barry Lawrence, Librarian, for their help and encouragement; Mr. Michael Bayley for the use of his reconstructions numbered 6, 11, 13 and 14; Dr. Grenville Astill for the use of his map of medieval Maidenhead, no. 15; Mr. Donald Young for the photograph of All Saints' church, no. 70; and finally Maidenhead Library for the use of photographs from their collection, nos. 1, 2, 4, 5, 7, 8, 17, 20, 22, 24, 25, 27, 30, 31, 33-35, 37-54, 56, 57, 61, 63, 64, 66-69, 72-74, 78, 81, 83-85, 89-92, 95-107, 109-114, 118-122, 128-133, 135-152, many of which were presented by the *Maidenhead Advertiser* and the people of the town. All other illustrations are from the author's collection.

Historical Introduction

The town of Maidenhead is situated in east Berkshire on the A4 trunk road from London to Bristol and, whilst it would be correct to say that it lies within the Thames valley, it would not be strictly accurate to call it Maidenhead-on-Thames. Unlike the neighbouring settlements of Windsor, Reading, Henley and Marlow, where the towns are built on the banks of the river, the centre of Maidenhead is some three-quarters of a mile from the river bridge, for reasons which will later become apparent.

Be that as it may, before the town was built in the 13th century the river had always proved an attraction for early settlers. Over the past million years a succession of ice ages, glacial and inter-glacial periods, had carved out the Thames valley, leaving a series of terraces on which the people of the Old Stone Age settled. Living in rough shelters and using artefacts of bone and stone, these hunter-gatherers left behind a legacy of stone axes which have been found during gravel extraction in the locality. Maidenhead is famous for its hand axes, found in large numbers at Boyn Hill and Nightingale Pit, Furze Platt.

Most tributaries of the Thames show occupation during the Middle Stone Age after 10,000 B.C., when the climate became warmer and the area more thickly wooded. These hunter-fishermen settled close by the water's edge to avoid attack by wild animals, and fishing was an important part of their economy. They therefore designed primitive wooden boats and a series of small flint implements to use when spearing fish. Some 10,000 of these flint microliths were found in excavations by the Cut at Braywick in 1972 together with some Thames picks, a type of hand axe.

Clearance of the forest began in 4,000 B.C. when the Neolithic peoples brought knowledge of farming to Britain. Their stone tools were of a more sophisticated design, with axes smoothed by polishing and intricate arrowheads. They introduced cereals to the area and the very first round-based pottery which was used for both cooking and storage. At Canon Hill, Bray, Neolithic pottery from hearths gave a radiocarbon date of 3320 B.C., perhaps the earliest date for ceramics in Britain. This early date may also indicate that both Neolithic and Mesolithic peoples lived side by side for a short period.

Evidence of the ensuing Bronze and Iron Ages is to be found in the form of hut circles and farming complexes on or near to the Thames flood plain, notably at Bray and Furze Platt. Multivallate hillforts from the early Iron Age occur on the higher ground at Medmenham, Easthampstead and High Wycombe, but not in the immediate locality. There is, however, considerable evidence of the Belgae of the late Iron Age who settled in the Thames Valley just prior to the Roman invasion. One local earthwork on Maidenhead Thicket, known locally as Robin Hood's Arbour, was excavated in 1959 and proved to be an animal enclosure dated between A.D. 1-50. A linear earthwork at Thicket Corner, investigated in 1982, is thought to be a boundary ditch of the same complex.

During the Romano-British period the land around Maidenhead was given over to the cultivation of cereals to feed the army in Wales and the north. Villa farms occurred at one-and-a-half mile intervals, each with their own allocation of land on which tax was paid to the Roman overlords at the *civitas* capital Calleva, south of Reading. A dozen villas are known in the local area, two of which are situated within Maidenhead borough.

Part of Saxton's map of Berkshire, 1574.

The first of these was excavated in the garden of 'The Firs', Castle Hill, by James Rutland in 1886, and revealed a suite of baths with furnaces and underfloor heating. A more scientific investigation was carried out on the second, which was located in Northumbria Road, Cox Green, and was first spotted in 1960 on an aerial photograph. This building showed an occupation from the first to the fourth centuries A.D. and had 20 rooms which included a suite of baths.

There was no Roman settlement at Maidenhead, but there may have been one at Cookham where the elusive Camlet Way, linking the Roman towns of St Albans and Silchester, crossed the Thames. Another supposed Roman road from Braywick to Cookham passes through the town of Maidenhead and is clearly visible in Kidwells Park. There may also have been a small settlement at Bray where in 1970 a large fifth-century cemetery produced 100 skeletons and some cremations.

Most settlements in east Berkshire were formed during the Anglo-Saxon era when the Thames served as a natural barrier between Wessex and Mercia. Many villages nearer the river have the suffix -ham (settlement), whilst others with the suffix -field originated as clearings in the Forest of Windsor, used for hunting by the Norman kings. Prior to the building of Windsor Castle in 1070, the royal palace of Edward the Confessor was situated at Old Windsor, which gave the whole area the status of a royal borough. This included Maidenhead's parent manors Cookham and Bray, which were always royal manors held by the king.

Cookham itself was probably an important frontier town. We have evidence of a monastery there by A.D. 700 and the Witan met there under Ethelred the Unready in 997. The island of Sashes at Cookham has now been identified as the site of Sceaftsege, an Alfredian fort listed in the Burghal Hideage. Many Saxon burials have been discovered there, some in flat graves as at Rowborough, and others in re-used burial mounds on Cockmarsh.

As in most areas Saxon dwellings do not seem to have survived, probably because they were made of perishable materials. However, one group excavated at Holyport in 1972 was preserved in peat and yielded wooden stakes and brushwood floors with grass-marked pottery typical of the period. This site was dated by radiocarbon to about A.D. 753.

Without doubt the most spectacular finds of the period were made in 1883 in the burial mound of Taeppa which stands in the grounds of Taplow Court above Maidenhead Bridge. The skeleton of the chief, which was adorned with gold braid, was accompanied by grave goods also mainly of gold, including drinking horns, buckles, clasps, brooches and dresswear. These finds are on display in the British Museum and are rated second only to the treasure found at Sutton Hoo.

Whilst the town of Maidenhead as built on its present site dates to the 13th century, the origins of the settlement go back to Domesday and beyond. In 1086 the town is recorded in the great survey as follows:

> Giles holds *Elentone*. Siward held it before 1066. Then and now for 3 hides. Land for 4 ploughs. Two men, Hugh and Landri, hold from Giles; they have 2 ploughs. 6 villagers and 4 cottagers with one plough. Meadow 16 acres; woodland at 10 pigs. The value was 60 shillings, now 40 shillings.

The site of Elentone lies one mile to the north of the present town, in the area known appropriately as North Town. Of the Saxon owner, Siward, we know little unless he is an early Abbot of Chertsey; but Giles' full name is Giles de Pinkney, which derives from Picquigny on the Somme and is perpetuated in the local settlement of Pinkney's Green.

He was a Norman knight of some importance, well liked by William I, and rewarded for his part in the Conquest with considerable lands in Northamptonshire. It is unlikely that he ever lived at Elentone, and this is supported by the fact that he had two subtenants, Hugh and Landri, to look after his affairs.

From the Domesday text it would appear that Elentone comprised 360 acres of land, with 16 acres of meadow, 300 acres of arable land and enough woodland to support 10 pigs. The population can be calculated at about 42 people, made up mainly of manorial workers dependent on the lord of the manor for their livelihood.

Fortunately, we have considerable evidence of this site from excavations carried out between 1966 and 1972, which were co-directed by the author. An examination of a central platform located within a triple moat revealed structures and occupation debris from the 11th to the 16th centuries. The main building was a Norman longhouse with flint and chalk foundations and evidence of wattle and daub construction. Other features included a stable, a kitchen area, an industrial complex and two wells packed tight with medieval pottery and metal objects. In later medieval times the site of Elentone developed into the Cookham manor of Spencers and Knight Ellington, eventually dwindling into the modern Spencers Farm.

Soon after 1200 a small settlement grew up on the borders of Cookham and Bray on the site of the present town of Maidenhead. Until the year 1296 this village is recorded in the Bray court rolls as South Aylington, which despite its spelling obviously derived from Domesday Elentone, being situated to its south. It was a settlement of little importance and very much a backwater ignored by the outside world. This soon changed when a wooden bridge was built across the Thames, putting the hamlet on the very busy route from London to Bristol.

The bridge was to prove a lifeline to the town, and the main reason for its subsequent development. Like most early bridges it was built of timber, mainly oaks from the Forest of Windsor. It was certainly standing by 1255, when Henry III issued an order for widening the road between the bridge and Henley to counteract attacks by robbers, but it may well have been in position 50 years earlier. It regularly fell into disrepair and many grants, including one by Edward I in 1297, were made for major repairs.

The hamlet of South Aylington was situated, as Maidenhead is today, some three-quarters of a mile from the river. Research has shown that the flood plain from Cookham to Bray was liable to annual flooding and that early settlements tended to be sited just above the level of the water. Accordingly, when the bridge was erected a causeway was built to link the river with the hamlet, which later became Bridge Road.

Alongside the bridge a timber wharf was erected for the storage and transportation of oaks from the Forest of Windsor. Some of the timber was obviously used for continuous repairs to the bridge, whilst surplus quantities were shipped as far as London and Oxford. We have no early description of this structure but the antiquary Leland, when passing through in 1538, recorded that he 'came to Maidenhead Bridge of timber upon the Thames and there was great wharfage of timber and firewood on the west end of the bridge; and this wood comes out of Berkshire and the great woods and forest of Windsor'. Again, in 1675, Ogilby stated that 'Maidenhead has a well frequented market, and a quay, to which barges come from London'. The wharf is also shown to be extant in an engraving of about 1750.

It was from this New Wharf or 'Maiden Hythe' that the town of Maidenhead eventually took its name, from the year 1297 onwards. The earliest version of the word is 'Maideheg', c.1202, which may mean that the wharf was in existence at this time, and perhaps even the bridge. No less than 33 spellings of the name were recorded before the present version came into use in 1724.

> After the men of Maidenhead had built here a wooden bridge upon piles, it [the town] began to have inns and be so frequented as to outvie its neighbouring mother Bray, a much more ancient place.

These words were written by the antiquary Camden who visited Maidenhead in the 16th century, and indicate the importance of the bridge to the economy of the town. The inhabitants had been quick to react to the consistent stream of travellers passing through, and provided inns, alehouses, stabling and smithies to accommodate their needs. Maidenhead was one day's journey from London and a convenient stopping point. Even the footpads recognised the potential and assembled on Maidenhead Thicket for the purpose of robbing those travelling the route to Bristol or Gloucester.

The bridge itself provided a source of income to the town, and from an early period tolls were collected from travellers. There is a record of a small hermitage on the west end of the bridge being rebuilt as a tollgate in 1423, and of one Richard Ludlow being appointed to collect tolls. Maidenhead bridge remained a toll-bridge until 1903, when the gates were ceremoniously thrown into the river.

The medieval town stretched from Castle Hill to the bottom of the High Street with one back lane, now West Street. There was further occupation in Bridge Street, which was separated from the High Street by a second wooden bridge crossing the Dunmede stream, first mentioned in 1380 by a monk of St Denys. This stream was once quite wide and possibly navigable but it has now dwindled to the modern York stream and is bridged by the brick-built Chapel Arches, most of which is now covered with shops.

Chapel Arches derives its name from the chapel-at-ease which was erected nearby by the Hosebund family in 1270 to cater for travellers. This chapel was also welcomed by the locals, who until that time had to walk to either the church at Cookham or at Bray, which proved very difficult in times of flood. However, the vicars of these churches saw the new chapel as a threat to their income and appealed to the bishop, who refused to allow the church to be used officially for worship until the year 1324. In 1352 John Hosebund left in his will £100 for a 'chauntry and one priest' and the new building was dedicated to St Andrew and St Mary Magdalene. This was the forerunner of the borough church of St Mary's and was rebuilt in 1724, 1824 and 1963.

The Market Square was situated centrally in the High Street where it meets Market Street. This area used to be much wider, with the guildhall, built in 1777 and demolished 20 years ago, set back on the south side. An earlier market hall stood on this site, with an open ground floor which accommodated a corn market. On the north side of the square was the *Swan Inn*, used by market traders for refreshments and for settling their accounts.

Throughout the early medieval period the settlement of Maidenhead came under the jurisdiction of the manors of Cookham and Bray. Other manors were formed by sub-infeudation during the 13th century and most of the land surrounding the town was owned by four manorial estates. To the north of the High Street, the old Domesday site of Elentone became the manor of Spencers and Knight Ellington and administered the lands by the river. To the west of this, the new manor of Pinkneys covered the rest of the Cookham land. To the south of the town lands stretching from the river to Boyn Hill were owned by the manor of Ives, with the manor house standing on the site of the present town hall. The adjoining lands of Cox Green were owned by the manor of Ockwells or Ockholt, once a hunting lodge in Windsor Forest. The manor house of Ockwells stands today and is a fine example of 15th-century architecture.

Maidenhead's first charter of incorporation was granted in 1582, but some sort of corporate life existed in 1452 with the formation of the guild of St Andrew and St Mary Magdalene. The guild was formed after Thomas Mettingham, priest of the chauntry in Maidenhead chapel, made application to Henry VI, and it comprised an overseer with wardens, brethren and sisters. They were charged with the maintenance of the chauntry and perpetual repairs to Maidenhead bridge, which regularly fell down. They were empowered to elect two wardens annually and other brethren and sisters as required, and have a common seal. They met at the guildhall, but like all similar institutions were dissolved by Henry VIII in 1547.

After 30 years Sir Henry Neville applied to Queen Elizabeth I for the re-establishment of the guild. This resulted in the official charter of incorporation whereby the town became a separate entity and broke its ties with the manors of Cookham and Bray. The corporation was to comprise one warden, two bridgemasters and eight burgesses, who were elected annually in September. These men had the power to create laws, statutes, ordinances and constitutions and to possess lands. Their jurisdiction was over the entire area with the boundary of 'Maydenheth' which was described as extending 'from the Bridge to Braywick, to Boyne Hill and to the Courthouse, and then to North Town and back to the Bridge'.

The importance of the bridge to the prosperity of the town is again emphasised by the appointment of bridgemasters, and by the fact that the charter provided a new scale of tolls for merchandise and vehicles passing over the structure. A second charter was granted by James I in 1604, and others in 1662 and 1685. The final charter raised the warden to the rank of mayor and granted permission for a high steward and a town clerk to be elected. The first mayor of Maidenhead was Vincent Pawlyn, who was elected in 1685.

During the next 200 years Maidenhead increased little in size, but attained a new importance with the introduction of stage and private coaches. By 1750 traffic on what by now had become the Bath Road had increased considerably until, in its heyday, there were 90 coaches a day passing through the town. The wooden bridge had been reinforced several times because of this additional traffic and the final repair in 1750 cost £764. Plans for a stone bridge were submitted to the corporation by Robert Taylor, and the present structure was built just south of the old bridge and opened to the public on 22 August 1777. Since that date the bridge has required little maintenance.

Most stage coaches were heavy, and up to six horses had to be changed every 10 miles. A coach only held six passengers, so the expensive journey was made mainly by the middle classes, while the rich travelled in their own vehicles or privately-hired post-chaises. New trades grew up in the town to cater for the needs of these long-distance travellers and by 1830 it was recorded that there were three blacksmiths, two coachmakers, three saddlers and harness-makers, two wheelwrights, two veterinary surgeons, one whipmaker and one livery stable keeper in the town. In a survey carried out in 1834, it was shown that over a period of two weeks 823 coaches passed through the town, using 3,000 horses. It has been claimed that Maidenhead had more coaches passing through than any other town in England.

A large area of the town was given over to coaching inns with gardens and stables. Apart from the *Orkney Arms* by the bridge, there were the *Red Lion* and the *Bear Inn* in the lower High Street, and the *Saracens Head* and the *White Hart* in the upper part. One of the largest inns was the *Sun*, which was situated at the bottom of Castle Hill. It had a 62-ft.

frontage with a handsome portico and stabling for 40 horses. The inn supplied 'cock' horses, as in the nursery rhyme, to help pull westbound coaches up the steep hill.

The *Greyhound Inn*, which once stood on the site of the National Westminster Bank in the High Street, burnt down in 1735, but not before playing its part in the town's history. On 16 July 1647 it was the scene of an historic event when Charles I was re-united with his children for the last time before his execution, 18 months later. The same inn played host to the Quaker, Thomas Ellwood, in spring 1660 when he was arrested for riding his horse through the town on a Sunday, and was imprisoned at the inn until the following morning. However, as the Quaker had no money, the warden had to foot the bill, much to his disgust! Perhaps it was here too that Sir Walter Raleigh's trial was held in 1603 because the judges wished to avoid the plague that was raging in London.

There were also numerous alehouses in the town, some notorious like the *Bull* and the *Fighting Cocks* which were frequented by drunken soldiers who were always being thrown out on their necks. The supply of beer was inexhaustible, as Maidenhead had four breweries. The oldest was Langton's in West Street, and the others were Bell's or Fuller's in Bell Street, Keys in Keys Lane and Nicholson's, which outlasted all the others. Nicholson's brewery was built on the site of the old *White Hart Inn* and is now a shopping precinct.

It was during the Victorian period that major changes took place in Maidenhead. In 1801 it was still a small town of 949 inhabitants but by 1851 the population had risen to 3,603. A lot happened in between these two dates, not the least of which was the coming of the railway. Plans for the iron road began in 1835 when the Great Western Railway was formed and Maidenhead was seen as the first terminus on the line.

Isambard Kingdom Brunel was appointed as the G.W.R. engineer and he completed the first section of the line to Maidenhead in three years. The earliest station was Maidenhead Riverside, situated on the Buckinghamshire bank of the river where the line terminated because there was no bridge across the Thames. The station was of a temporary nature and had an associated engine shed designed and built by Daniel Gooch, a local man from Clewer, who was later knighted and elected chairman of the G.W.R.

The first train ran from Paddington to Maidenhead on 31 May 1838, pulled by the Stephenson locomotive *North Star*, which had been brought by barge and unloaded at Maidenhead bridge. The line was officially opened to the public on 4 June and 1,479 people travelled that day, paying a total of £226 in fares. In the following year Brunel's famous railway bridge spanning the Thames was completed and the line continued to Reading and ultimately to Bristol. The bridge is world famous for its wide brick spans of 128 feet and is still standing after 150 years despite criticism from Brunel's rivals.

A second station known as Maidenhead Boyn Hill was erected between Castle Hill and Grenfell Road in 1854 and this, together with Riverside, was in use until 1871 when the present station opened. The immediate effect of the railway on the inhabitants was one of gloom. For several hundred years they had relied on travellers and the coaching trade for their livelihood, and now it was being phased out. Almost everyone in the town was affected, and even the footpads on the Thicket faced redundancy. Maidenhead corporation was forced to lower its bridge tolls to counteract the railway, and this action together with the reduced road traffic drastically reduced the town's income. Even the short-term subsidy offered by the G.W.R. was no compensation once the coaches stopped in 1843.

However, from time the Thames was bridged by the railway in 1839 there was an influx of middle-class commuters who saw the chance of living in a rural area within striking distance of the capital. The population of the town almost quadrupled in three years so that by 1841 the inhabitants numbered 3,815, a higher total than in 1851. The demands of this new population attracted businessmen and entrepreneurs from London who bought up redundant properties in the town centre and converted them into shops and business premises. Most of them had no desire to live above their place of work, as the working-class Maidonians had done, and commissioned villas to be built for them on Castle Hill and at Norfolk Park. The first phases of building were carried out by small builders on an *ad hoc* basis, but as housing demands increased a handful of local developers were inspired to form the Maidenhead Improvement Company in the early 1860s and set about extending the area for the new residents. Maidenhead began to expand in all directions and many new streets appeared. By 1875 Queen Street and King Street had been erected as new shopping streets, with Victoria, Albert and Princess Streets, Broadway, York Road, Park Street and Grove Road providing affordable housing. More elegant houses were built in the Boyn Hill area and Charles Butler, the working man's friend, erected houses in Cordwallis Road, Denmark Street, Reform Road and Waldeck.

Many fashionable residences also sprang up by the riverside. The new railway brought hoards of tourists, playboys and debutantes to the river, and the Maidonians, as usual, rose to the occasion. The *Orkney Arms* was converted to *Skindle's*, an hotel that gained an international reputation and was popular with celebrities and royalty after Edward VII dined there while mingling with high society at Taplow Court and Cliveden. The *Riviera*, *Thames* and *Ray Mead* hotels were built to satisfy public demand and seedy clubs like Murrays and the Hungaria provided doubtful entertainment. Maidenhead became a weekend place with a reputation for scandal. A popular quip of the time was 'are you married or do you live in Maidenhead?'

Prosperous landowners like William Grenfell, later Lord Desborough of Taplow Court, donated lands for parks and public buildings. Among the middle-class there was a demand for better schools and more churches. St Mary's, which had been the only Anglican church for 600 years, was supplemented by All Saints, St Luke's, St Peter's and St Paul's, together with the Catholic church of St Joseph and chapels for other denominations. The first public library opened in 1904 and was erected with a donation from the Carnegie Trust.

As the new century dawned, Maidenhead was still a popular riverside resort with an increased population of 12,980. This was somewhat reduced during the First World War, and the names of those who gave their lives are recorded on the war memorial in St Ives Road. For those who survived, 'homes fit for heroes' were provided in the form of the first council houses in Ellington Park and Australia Avenue.

To a certain extent development came to a standstill between the two World Wars. During the Second World War Maidenhead was affected by the bombing, mainly due to its proximity to White Waltham aerodrome. There was a large influx of evacuees, the most famous of whom was Queen Wilhelmina of the Netherlands who stayed in Stubbings House. By 1948 the town's population was 26,790 with 7,326 houses, and by 1965 this had increased to 41,230 with 12,444 houses. Since 1945 nearly 2,000 council houses have been erected on estates at Halifax Road, Curls Lane and Wessex Way. Similarly, a further 5,000 private homes have been built at Highway, Cannon Lane and Furze Platt. Building has now reached its limit without encroaching on the Green Belt.

The latter expansion was mainly due to the establishment of Maidenhead as a commuter town. Improved railway services and the opening of the M4 motorway made communications with London much easier and encouraged people to settle in the town where housing was not cheap but nevertheless cheaper than in the capital. Today Maidenhead has more cars per family than most places, and the ring road built around the town's perimeter has helped to relieve the congestion which was endemic during holiday periods.

Flooding was a hazard in Maidenhead and used to occur nearly every year. The worst years were 1894, 1903, and 1947 when the water reached the edge of the town, leaving half a mile of flooded buildings in its wake. In recent years a flood relief ditch has been excavated, which so far seems to have helped the problem.

The old guildhall was eventually demolished and the present town hall opened in 1962 by the Queen and Prince Philip. In her speech the Queen referred to previous royal visits:

> There is a story that when James I was once stranded here without any money, the curate paid for his dinner and was promptly made Canon of Windsor. When Charles II came here the Corporation indulged in a dinner which cost one pound fifteen shillings. I am afraid that your entertainment to me today is going to cost a little more and I hope that you will not ask the vicar to pay for it!

The town hall remained the administrative centre when the boundaries changed in 1974 and the town became part of the Royal Borough of Windsor and Maidenhead.

Today Maidenhead has very few ancient buildings and is a far cry from the 'street of inns' and the market town of medieval times. Hi-tech industries have moved in, making the area part of the so-called Silicon Valley, and a large proportion of the town is now given over to office blocks. The population is around 60,000, many of whom work outside the area. Maidenhead has had to move with the times, like so many towns in England.

The Plates

Inches

1. An Old Stone Age axe found in gravels at Maidenhead. Artefacts of this type have been discovered in large numbers in Thames terraces, notably at Furze Platt and Boyn Hill.

2. This socketed spearhead dredged from the Thames near the Sounding Arch provides evidence of early metal users.

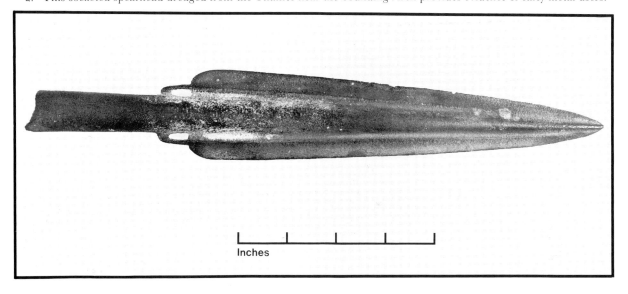

Inches

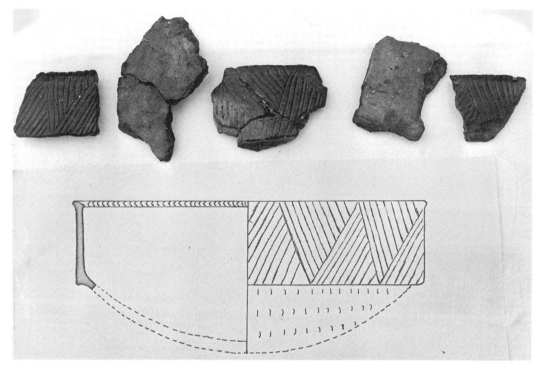

3. Secondary Neolithic pottery dated 2000 B.C. as used by the New Stone Age farmers. It was excavated from a contemporary hearth at The Binghams, Canon Hill, Braywick.

4. Robin Hood's Arbour, Maidenhead Thicket. The site is a ditched animal enclosure of the Belgic period and was dated between A.D. 1-50 when excavated in 1959.

5. Mr. James Rutland excavating the furnaces of a Roman Villa near the corner of Castle Hill and Grenfell Road in 1886.

6. A reconstruction of the Cox Green Roman Villa as it was in about A.D. 100. This building was located in Northumbria Road and was fully excavated in 1960. The villa was in use from the first to the fourth centuries and had an extensive baths suite. Outbuildings from the villa complex have been found in Altwood Bailey.

7. Taplow Court, built around 1850 by the Grenfell family. In the foreground is the Saxon burial mound of the chieftain Taeppa after whom the village is named. This was excavated in 1883 and yielded a treasure which is on display in the British Museum. The graveyard once belonged to the church of St Nicholas which was demolished in 1828 when the present parish church was built in the village.

8.   Spencers Farm, Cookham Road, as it was in 1960. The name derives from the medieval family of Despenser, ancestors of the Princess of Wales, who held the Manor of Spencers and Knight Ellington. It stood on land belonging to the Domesday Manor of Elentone in 1086. It is now a housing estate with the principal road Aldebury signifying an ancient town.

9.   Excavations on the Domesday site of Elentone at Spencers Farm took place between 1966 and 1972, yielding the first evidence of Maidenhead as it was in the 11th century. The photograph shows Dr. C. F. Slade (*left*) and the author who co-directed the dig.

10. Another view of the Domesday site of Elentone. A platform within a triple moat was explored to reveal foundations of a Norman hall, being the residence of the lord of the manor. The foundations were of chalk and flint.

11. A reconstruction, based on the excavations, of the moated manor house of Elentone with ancillary buildings. The satellite settlement where the peasants lived lies just beyond.

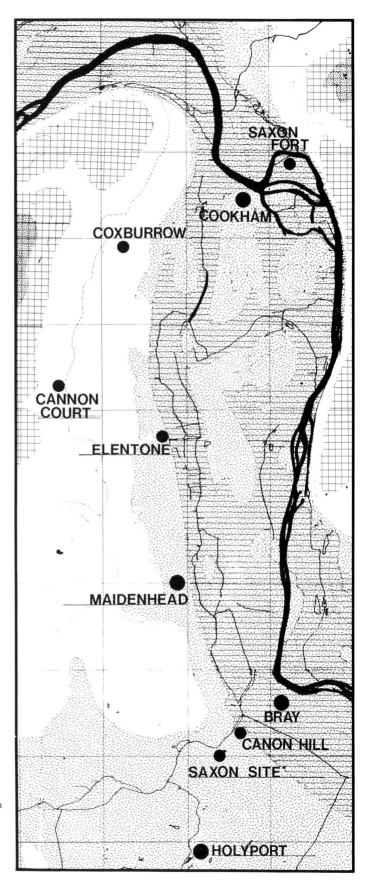

12. A map showing the large flood plain between Cookham and Bray. Because of this hazard, key settlements were situated just above the plain. There is some evidence that at one time the villages of Cookham and Bray were located away from the river.

13. By the year 1255 the first wooden bridge had been built across the Thames at Maidenhead, putting the town firmly on the map. This bridge, providing a through-route to Bristol, is clearly illustrated in this reconstruction of the riverside in 1582.

14. The chapel of St Andrew and St Mary Magdalene was built in the centre of the road outside the present *Bear Hotel* in 1270. It straddled the borders of the two parent manors, Cookham and Bray, so that each side of the chapel was in a different parish. This reconstruction shows the other wooden bridge at Maidenhead known as Chapel Arches, crossing the Dunmede stream.

MAIDENHEAD - medieval features

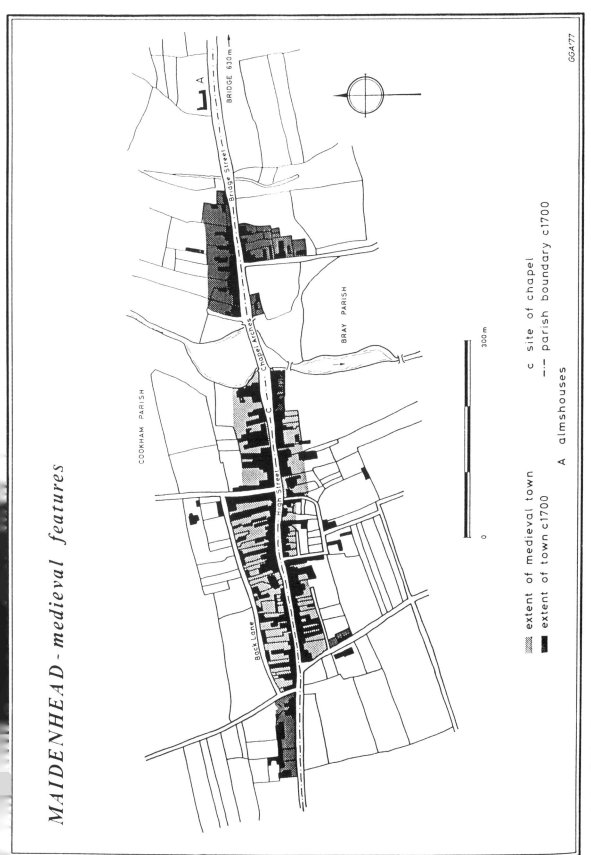

COOKHAM PARISH

Back Lane

High Street

Chapel Arches

BRAY PARISH

Bridge Street

BRIDGE 630 m

A

GGA'77

0   300 m

▨ extent of medieval town   c site of chapel

■ extent of town c1700   --- parish boundary c1700

A almshouses

15. A plan of Maidenhead showing the extent of the town in medieval times. It was basically one street with a back lane (now West Street). There is a break in the building line where the Dunmede stream flows under Chapel Arches.

16.   The oldest building in the town, situated on the corner of Moorbridge Road and Forelease Road. This was originally the *Jolly Gardeners* alehouse and then the *Gardeners Arms*. During renovation in 1989 the roof beams dating to *c*.1550-80 could clearly be seen.

17.   As building work progresses in Maidenhead, foundations of medieval dwellings are often recorded. In this picture Elias Kupferman (*left*) and the author are examining early chalk walls on a site in Market Street.

18. Ives Place painted between 1810 and 1825 by Anne Pocock. This rural scene belies the fact that the building now lies beneath the town hall, and that the grassy bank sloping down to the Dunmede is the site of the library in St Ives Road. Ives Place started its life as the manor house of Ives, situated in Bray parish since 1296. The manor of Ives held land extending as far as Boyn Hill.

19. The Ives mansion just before demolition in 1957. In the 16th century it was the property of Queen Anne of Cleves, and had many owners before William Wilberforce changed its name to St Ives Place in 1870. By 1923 it was the *St Ives Hotel* and, later, local government offices.

20.   Ockwells Manor, Cox Green, is one of the finest examples of its kind in southern England. Built in the 1440s by the Norreys family, it is now restored and in private ownership. The Manor of Ockwells or Ockholt can be traced back to 1267, when it was probably a hunting lodge in the Windsor Forest.

21.   Although the Manor of Shoppenhangers can be traced back to 1288, the present building, despite its ancient appearance, was erected in 1915 by Walter Thornton-Smith, an antiques dealer. It is presently a restaurant for the *Crest Hotel*.

VIVAT REGINA

E R

regina fi
ibidem
bonis
haberi
wittg̃ p̃dc̃
predicti
nostri ge
apptinet 2
pontem
voluin

habens pcquircud̃ũ
termino vite vitay et annoy seu aliter quouisuio
nomen Gardiani Pontentrioy Burgensium et Co
Insticiariis ac aliis psssonis et officiariis nostris
forma prout alii ligei nostri huius regni nostri
possint Et quod predc̃ Gardianus pontent̃ Burg

22. Maidenhead's Charter of Incorporation issued by Queen Elizabeth I in 1582. From this date the town became a separate entity and broke its ties with the manors of Cookham and Bray.

23. The original plan for the Guildhall erected in 1777. Earlier market halls had been built in a similar style, with the ground floor housing the cornmarket.

24. The Guildhall when completed, set back to form a market square. The corner shop and post office stands on the site of the old *Bear Inn*, and is now occupied by the Midland Bank.

25.   A scene outside the Guildhall in 1901 when the mayor, William Good, proclaimed the death of Queen Victoria.

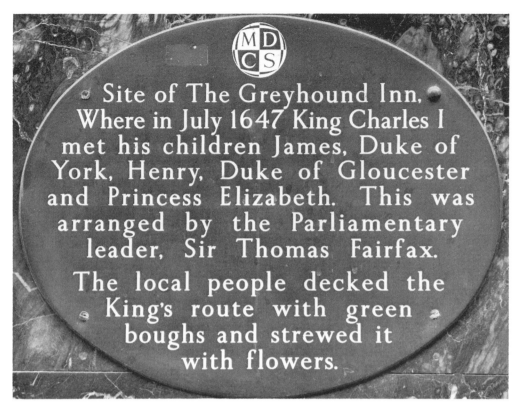

The plaque reads:

Site of The Greyhound Inn, Where in July 1647 King Charles I met his children James, Duke of York, Henry, Duke of Gloucester and Princess Elizabeth. This was arranged by the Parliamentary leader, Sir Thomas Fairfax.

The local people decked the King's route with green boughs and strewed it with flowers.

26.   A plaque outside the Nat West Bank, High Street, commemorating the visit of Charles I. The *Greyhound*, one of Maidenhead's earliest inns, was burnt down in 1735.

27.   This building, outlined at the time of demolition, was originally the *Sun* coaching inn at the base of Castle Hill. In its heyday the inn had stabling for 40 horses and supplied 'cock' horses to help pull coaches up Castle Hill.

28. The *White Hart* was situated in the centre of Maidenhead High Street opposite Woolworth's. Its stabling and gardens occupied the site of Nicholson's shopping precinct before the brewery was built.

29. The *Boar's Head*, now the *Longbeach*, stands on the site of the *Red Lion* coaching inn in the lower High Street. In 1636 it was bought by the Mattingly family, who for a short time used it as a cornmarket.

30. The Salter's almshouses in Bridge Road, built by James Smyth in 1659.

THEIS ALMESHOWSES WERE EREC
TED & BVILT AT Y SOLE & PROPER
COST & CHARGES OF JAMES SMYTH
ESQVIOR CITIZEN & SALTER OF
LONDON in y̅ yeare of our lord 1659

31. The decorative plaque over the door of the Salter's almshouses.

32. Maidenhead's first stone bridge across the Thames as seen in 1780. This bridge, designed by Robert Taylor, replaced a series of wooden bridges which were regularly falling down. It was opened to the public in 1777.

33. Maidenhead Bridge in 1797 showing the *Orkney Arms*, later *Skindle's*, on the right. Bridge House, on the west bank, stands on the site of Bridge Gardens.

34. Maidenhead Bridge in 1895 showing the *Riviera Hotel* on the left, and the toll gates leading to Bridge Street.

35. The toll gates in Bridge Street at the turn of the century. Tolls had been collected from those crossing the bridge since at least 1423, but were discontinued in 1903 when the toll gates were ceremoniously thrown into the river.

36. There was also a toll gate at Maidenhead Thicket on the route to Bath.

37.   The view towards Boulter's Lock from Maidenhead Bridge about 1835.

38.   Looking across at Bridge House from the Buckinghamshire bank. This house later became Murrays Club, before being demolished for the Hungaria Club. It is now Bridge Gardens.

39. The bridge and river about 1900
showing eel traps in the foreground and the
smaller bridge linking the Brigade of Guards
Club with its own island.

40. The Brigade of Guards Club in its
heyday, c.1890.

41. Skindle's Hotel by Maidenhead Bridge as it was in its earlier years. Originally it was the *Orkney Arms* but changed its name after William Skindle took it over in 1833. In the heyday of the river it was a fashionable place, often visited by members of royalty staying at Taplow Court or Cliveden.

42. Skindle's Hotel as we see it today.

43. The Bridge and the *Riviera Hotel* in 1912. The hotel building had been a mansion which was converted in 1888.

44. Boulter's Lock and Ray Mill House painted by Edmund Niemann in 1842. The lock had been built in 1830 as Ray Mill Pound, was extended in 1912 and again more recently. Boulter is not a personal name but refers to the bolter, or miller, who owned a flour mill there.

45. Ray Mills in 1910 just prior to demolition. They were situated adjacent to Boulter's Lock, and manufactured flour over a long period. The Ray family lived in Cookham for 700 years and owned most of the land by the river. The many Ray roads in this area were named after the family.

46. Boulter's Lock at the time of its rebuilding in 1912. Ray Mills have been demolished and the Mill House, now a hotel, is available for letting.

47. A photograph illustrating the popularity of
Boulter's Lock and the Thames earlier this century.
Large crowds could be seen at weekends and bank-
holidays.

48. The *Thames Hotel*, Ray Mead Road, in 1906. This hotel was built by the Woodhouse family in the 1880s in response to public demand for accommodation.

49. Before the Flood Relief Ditch was excavated in Maidenhead, floods were almost an annual occurrence, with the water reaching the bottom of the High Street. In this scene in February 1900 a ferry is operating in Bridge Road to deliver passengers to the almshouses.

50. A row of cottages on the Moor during the 1904 floods.

51. Floods came at the wrong time for this speculator who was trying to sell 'desirable' building plots on the Ray Lodge Estate!

52.　The whole area was under water in the last great flood which occurred in 1947.

53.　Floods reached the lower High Street in 1947 when evacuation was arranged.

54. The Congregational church was erected in West Street in 1785.

55. The old Congregational building still stands, but now called the United Reformed church. Although the exterior has been altered, the interior retains many of its original features.

56. Chapel Arches c.1810, showing the extreme width of the stream at that time. The water now runs through only one of the arches and has been renamed York Stream. Shops have now been built above the bridge. The church of St Andrew and St Mary Magdalene is seen in its original position in the centre of the road.

57. The church of St Andrew and St Mary Magdalene was moved and rebuilt on its present site in 1824. This building was demolished in the 1960s and the present modern church with a spire erected.

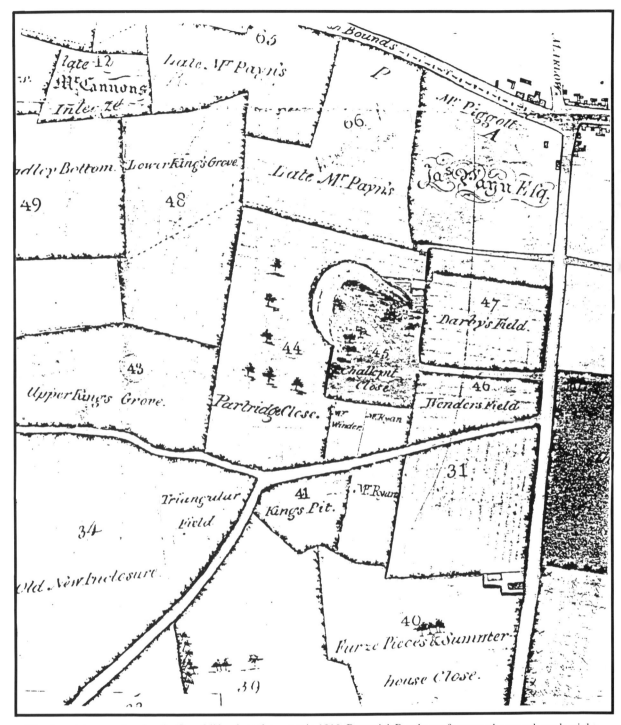

58.   An estate map showing the Grenfell lands as they were in 1810. Braywick Road runs from north to south on the right hand side whilst the lane from east to west is Shoppenhangers Road. Chalkpit Close equates to Grenfell Park.

59. A 1935 reconstruction of the *North Star* locomotive pulling the first train on the G.W.R. to Maidenhead Riverside terminus on 31 May 1838.

60. A unique photograph of Maidenhead Riverside station taken prior to demolition in 1871. The station was located on two levels and situated adjacent to the *Old Station Inn* at Taplow.

61. Brunel's brick-built railway bridge spanning the Thames at Maidenhead. The 128-ft. brick span arches are the widest in the world and were criticised when the bridge opened to traffic in 1839.

62. The railway brought crowds of visitors to the riverside at Maidenhead, as can be seen in this photograph of the Regatta in 1893.

63. Maidenhead Boyn Hill station which was located between Castle Hill and Grenfell Road. It was demolished in 1871 when the present station was opened.

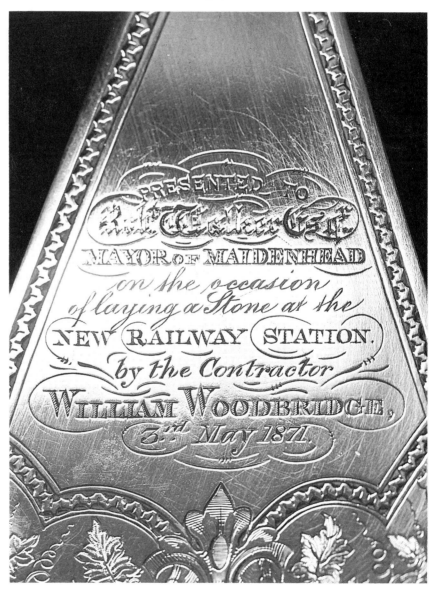

PRESENTED TO
R. J. Walker Esqr.
MAYOR OF MAIDENHEAD
on the occasion
of laying a Stone at the
NEW RAILWAY STATION,
by the Contractor
WILLIAM WOODBRIDGE,
3rd May 1871.

64. The trowel presented to the mayor of Maidenhead by William Woodbridge on 3 May 1871 on the occasion of laying a stone at the present railway station.

65.   The broad-gauge locomotive *Dragon* standing in Maidenhead station in 1880.

66.   Station Approach *c*.1904, showing passengers arriving for their train. The chimney in the centre belonged to Bells Brewery, Bell Street.

67. The Board Room of the Board of Guardians of the Maidenhead Union, erected in 1896. This building was an addition to the Cookham Workhouse or Poor Law Institution which opened in 1836.

68. Maidenhead Cottage Hospital in St Luke's Road before demolition in 1977. It was built in 1879 by public demand and extended in 1908 when the new wards were opened by H.R.H. Princess Christian. Additional wards were added in 1947.

69. St Joseph's Catholic church, Cookham Road, opened for worship in 1884 and replaced other Catholic chapels in the town.

70. All Saints' church, Boyn Hill, before the nave was extended in 1911. The buildings of the All Saints' complex are considered to be fine examples of Victorian architecture and are protected. The church was consecrated in 1857 by the Bishop of Oxford.

71. All Saints' church complex was designed by the architect G. E. Street, who produced this accurate impression before building commenced. It was originally designed to be built in stone but brick was substituted. Note the area of fields between the church and the town.

72. An early sketch of St Luke's church as it was at the time of opening in 1866 and before the spire was added.

73. Queen Anne House, Castle Hill, in 1970. It was built by Cooper's Brickworks and was intended to be a showcase for their products. Erected in 1880, it later became an hotel, then an annexe to the County Girls' School.

74. The Ice House, Castle Hill, in 1981. This Victorian house is reputed to be the earliest concrete building in England, and was erected by a Mrs. Hamblett over deep ice wells used by her fishmonger husband.

75. One of the ice wells in the cellars of the Ice House. Before refrigeration they were filled with ice from the Moor stream.

76. Langton's Folly, which once stood on the site of the Magnet Leisure Centre. This façade of Norman-style arches led nowhere and was built by tramps for John Langton, a local brewer, to obscure his view of the brewery malthouse.

77. Commissioned by Edwin Hewitt, a local draper, this castellated folly on Castle Hill was erected in 1897 using overcooked bricks and flints. The main building has triangular rooms while the garden contains a burial vault and is surrounded by a high wall and gatehouse.

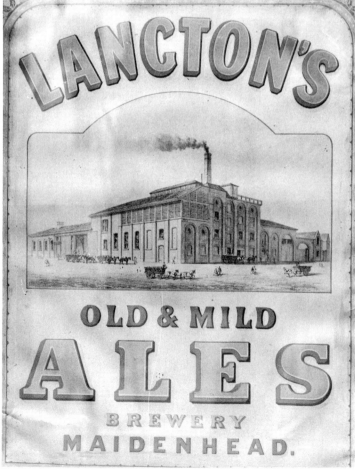

78.   Market Street looking towards the Guildhall, *c.*1826. This sketch illustrates the rural nature of the street at this time. There is a small farm with a haystack on the right alongside the buildings of Langton's, Maidenhead's oldest brewery.

79.   A poster advertising Langton's Brewery which stood on the corner of Market Street and West Street. Started in the 17th century, the premises were purchased by Nicholson's in 1906 and demolished in 1980.

80. Keys or East Berks. Brewery which still stands in Keys Lane, Grenfell Road. It came into being about 1833 and was taken over by Nicholson's in 1895. When in production it was linked to an off-licence in King Street.

81. Nicholson's Brewery towers above Moffatt Street and White Hart Road, an area of the town which has all been demolished. William Nicholson started his business in 1840 and erected his buildings over the stable and coach house area of the earlier *White Hart Inn*.

82. The entrance to Nicholson's Brewery from the High Street in the mid-19th century.

83. The Brewery entrance and offices about 1950, with the modern *White Hart* public house.

84.   A bunfight in Grenfell Park for Victoria's Jubilee in 1897. The park was presented to the town as a recreation ground by William Henry Grenfell in 1889. Originally it had been a chalkpit for the manufacture of lime.

85. The official opening of the Clock Tower, Station Approach, in 1900, which had been erected to celebrate the Diamond Jubilee of Queen Victoria.

86. The presentation of the 'Sir Roger' fire engine to the Maidenhead fire brigade by Lady Palmer in July 1919.

87. Stuchbery's Stores, established in 1760 in Maidenhead High Street. Part of the façade still exists above the shops of Burton's and McDonald's.

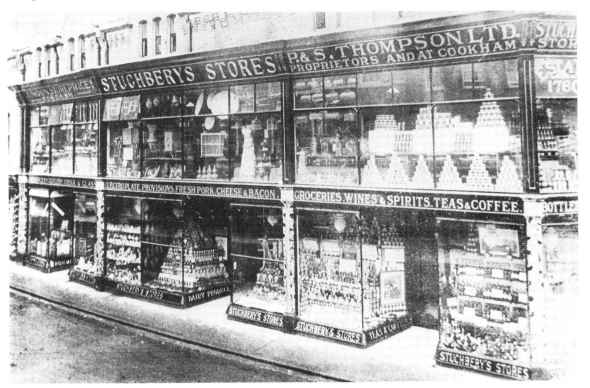

88. Watkins & Son, harness-makers in Market Street, with two of their customers.

89. Steane & Co., hardware merchants in King Street.

90. R. E. Plevey, family butchers, displaying their wares.

91. The Drill Hall in Marlow Road just before demolition in 1970. The building was a gift to the town from J. D. M. Pearce, a town benefactor, and was opened in 1903. Beyond it is the Art College which still stands.

92. Garden Cottages and allotments, c.1890. These were one of the concrete developments of J. D. M. Pearce and were situated east of the Cookham Road.

93. The county police station, Broadway, with Queen Street Green in the foreground. Built in 1857 on the corner of South Street, it housed the first properly-organised police force in Maidenhead.

94. The later Victorian-style police station, built in 1906 on the same spot as the county building. It was demolished in 1980 to make way for new high-rise buildings, by which time a new station had opened on the Moor.

95. Cullerns Passage, which leads from Broadway to Queen Street. This is part of an ancient way linking Maidenhead with Braywick.

96. Castle Hill, looking towards the town in 1906. The Ice House, Queen Anne House and the *Sun Inn* can be seen on the left.

97. The bottom of Castle Hill as it was in 1904. The Methodist church stands in the foreground at the junction of High Street and King Street.

98. The lower High Street in the early 20th century looking towards Chapel Arches.

MAIDENHEAD. HIGH STREET.

99. Maidenhead High Street *c*.1927 with the garden of 'Monkendens' on the left and Cresset Towers on the right.

100. The High Street at the junction of Queen Street, *c*.1906. The Guildhall stands on the right and the *Swan*, a market inn since 1489, on the left.

101. King Street looking towards High Street, *c.*1904, with Broadway Junction on the right.

102. The south end of King Street where it joins Station Approach, with the Jubilee Clock Tower and the *Bell Hotel*.

103. Queen Street from High Street, *c.*1904, showing the many elaborate buildings of the Victorian period.

104. Queen Street looking towards High Street, *c.*1900, with Truscott's Corn Store and the *Cliveden Temperance Hotel* on the right.

105. Bridge Street looking towards Chapel Arches, *c.*1906.

106. Bridge Road *c.*1906, looking towards the bridge.

107. Chapel Arches at the turn of the century, showing the Bridge Street Picture Theatre, the first of Maidenhead's cinemas. It was later the Ritz and is now the Berkshire Squash Club.

108. The Maidenhead roller-skating rink which was opened in 1910 by Mr. George Gude as part of a leisure complex. The building later became the Hippodrome and then the Arena. During the war the firm of A. Harvey, woodworkers, made flooring for Wellington bombers there. It is due for demolition in 1990.

109. The interior of the roller-skating rink in 1910.

110. Advertisements showing the varied use of the Arena building during its lifetime.

111.   Coronation Day 1911 at the corner of High Street and King Street.

112.   The Ada Lewis fountain being re-sited in Bridge Gardens. It was presented to the town in 1908 as a drinking trough and originally stood on the opposite side of the road near the *Riviera Hotel*.

113. An attractive picture of the *Two Brewers* public house on the corner of Marlow Road and High Street in 1904.

114.   The opening of the wooden cenotaph outside the *Bear Hotel* in 1919. This was a temporary monument and was replaced in 1920 by the present war memorial in St Ives Road.

115.   The mayor, T. W. Stuchbery, who started the legal firm, and Lord Desborough at the opening of the war memorial in 1920. Both of these gentlemen lost sons in the Great War.

Maidenhead Aerodrome

(Entrance from Windsor Road).

Proprietors: DONALD STEVENSON & Co., Ltd.

||||||||||||||||||||||||||||||||||||||||||||||||||||||||||||||||||||||||||||||||||||||||||||

A Grand Opening Display

OF

FLYING

On SATURDAY NEXT, June 8th,

AT 2 30 P.M.

HIS WORSHIP THE MAYOR (Councillor W. Archer),
supported by Members of the Town Council, has kindly
consented to open the Aerodrome. —————————

EXHIBITION FLIGHTS

BY WELL-KNOWN PILOTS

who have kindly offered to assist, including :

Capt. G. de HAVILLAND, O.B.E., A.F.C.,

designer of the famous " Moth " Light Aeroplane,

Capt. H. S. BROAD, A.F.C.,

Chief Test Pilot of the de Havilland Aircraft Cc., Ltd.

Capt. H. D. DAVIS, A.F.C.

Managing Director of the Brooklands School of Flying,

Capt. E. A. JONES & Major C. M. PICKTHORN, M.C.,

Instructors of the Brooklands School of Flying.

PASSENGER FLIGHTS

By the Instructors of the

BROOKLANDS SCHOOL OF FLYING

ENTRANCE TO GROUND 6d.   Cars Parked Free.

Refreshments by the "SPORTSMAN RESTAURANT."

||||||||||||||||||||||||||||||||||||||||||||||||||||||||||||||||||||||||||||||||||||||||||||

Phone : Maidenhead 1111.   Telegrams : " Planes, Maidenhead."

DONALD STEVENSON & Co., Ltd.,

Automobile & Aeronautical Engineers & Agents,

STATION APPROACH, MAIDENHEAD.

116.   An advertisement for the opening of Maidenhead Aerodrome in June 1929.

117. Alderman Cox makes a flight at the opening of Maidenhead Aerodrome at Bray in 1929.

118. The open-air swimming pool which was situated behind the leisure centre and demolished in 1989.

119.   The Maidenhead football club was founded in 1870, and was an ancestor of the present 'Magpies'. This photograph shows the team and managers in 1911.

120.   The Desborough bowling club in its early days.

121. The Hambletonian Hall, Market Street, *c.*1978. This hall stood on the site of Sainsbury's and was used for a variety of activities.

122. The Rialto cinema was opened in 1928 and was the largest of the town's three cinemas. It has now been demolished.

123. The opening programmes for all Maidenhead's cinemas. There were three actual buildings with six names.

124. Maidenhead's first-ever bus service which ran from the *Bear Hotel* to Streatley from 1915. The British bus service was started by Mr. Sidney Garcke of Pinkneys Green.

125. A Thornycroft double-decker bus travelling through the Maidenhead floods in 1925.

126. A changed landscape. Maidenhead bus station in Bridge Avenue, *c.*1957. The coach station lies beyond.

127. Marlow Road corner in the 1950s illustrating the traffic hold-ups which so often occurred.

128. (*above*) William Nicholson who founded the brewery in the mid-19th century. He lived on Castle Hill in the building later converted into the County Girls' School and which is now Castle Hill Centre.

129. (*above right*) J. Wesley Walker, an ex-mayor, alderman and J.P., who wrote the first history of Maidenhead in 1909, paving the way for later historians.

130. (*right*) Tom Middleton, editor of the *Maidenhead Advertiser* for many years, and author of three books about the area.

131. Local mayors gathered to greet Field Marshal Montgomery in the grounds of the Rialto cinema in 1945.

132. Serving personnel parade in Kidwells Park for Salute the Soldier Week, 1944.

133. The beating of the bounds ceremony, 1973. The last mayor of the Borough of Maidenhead, Mrs. E. Underhill, is bumped by Mr. John Smith, High Steward, and Dr. Alan Glyn, M.P. for the Borough. The two gentlemen have now been knighted.

134. Maidenhead church, U.S.A. The settlement of Maidenhead in America was founded by Quakers from Berkshire in 1698. The town has now been renamed Lawrenceville and was visited by Mrs. E. Underhill during the year she was mayor.

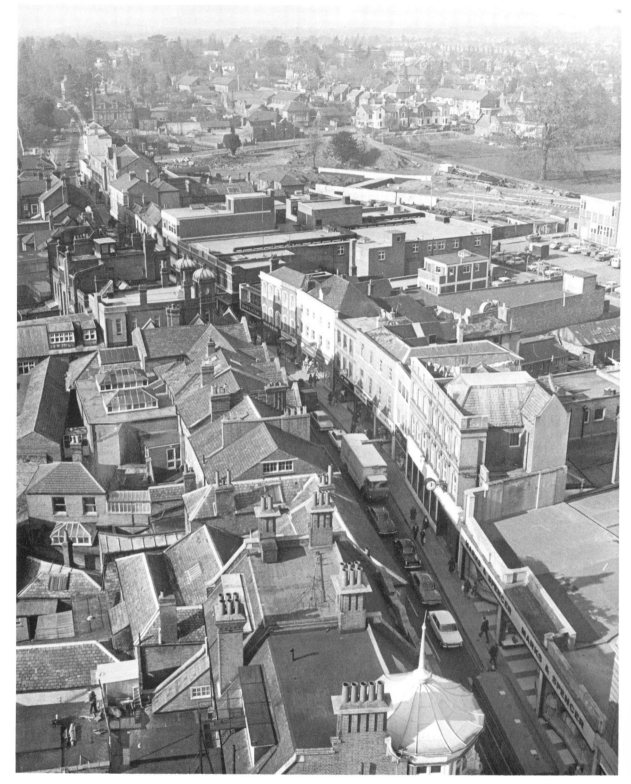

135. Aerial view of the High Street looking towards Castle Hill *c.*1971, when the bypass was being excavated.

136. Aerial view of Market Street and Cookham Road, *c.*1965.

137. The first stage of Nicholson's shopping precinct at night, *c*.1971.

138. The town hall for the Borough of Windsor and Maidenhead with Park Street in the foreground. It was opened in 1962 by H.M. the Queen and Prince Philip.

139. Maidenhead Library and 'Red' Square in St Ives Road. The building opened in 1973 and replaced the earlier Carnegie Library erected in 1904.

140. Aerial view of the Thames near Maidenhead and the Cliveden estate. Although Cliveden existed as a manor of Taplow in the 12th century, the first house was built in the 17th century by the Duke of Buckingham. The present house and estate were created in 1851 after the previous house had burnt down in both 1795 and 1849. Cliveden was the home of Lady Astor for many years and is now a hotel in National Trust grounds.

141. Aerial view of the Maidenhead road bridge and the Thames frontage to Boulter's Lock, 1946.

142. Aerial view of Maidenhead town showing the railway system, flood relief ditches and the relief road.

143. Her Majesty the Queen on a river trip from Henley to Windsor on 18 October 1974 with the mayor, Kit Aston.

144. The High Steward and his wife, now Sir John and Lady Smith, pass over the stewardship to H.R.H. Prince Charles after the formation of the Royal Borough of Windsor & Maidenhead in 1974.

145. Their Royal Highnesses Queen Elizabeth, the Queen Mother, and Princess Anne during the Silver Jubilee in 1977.

146. The Silver Jubilee procession in 1977 showing the Grimm Players float advertising 'Dick Turpin', a show written by the present author.

147. Bray village *c.*1890 showing the *Hinds Head Hotel* and the church.

148. Bray village from the church tower, *c.*1972.

149. Cookham village from the air.

150.   Cookham ferry and bridge in the 19th century. The Rev. William Scott and his son Walter land on Sashes Island.

151. Captain John Turk, the Queen's Swanmaster, who lives at Cookham riverside. The first swanmaster was appointed 600 years ago and members of the Turk family have held the position since 1922. Captain Turk officiates at the annual Swan-Upping ceremony which takes place every July, on which occasion the new cygnets are marked according to their ownership.

152. The late Stanley Spencer, well known modern artist and local character, who spent most of his life living and working in Cookham. The Spencer Art Gallery in the village has a large display of his better-known paintings.